10/04   27/8?   MN

W9-AUV-232

READING POWER

In the Ring with Bret Hart

Michael Payan

The Rosen Publishing Group's
PowerKids Press ™
New York

To Lynn...friends until the end

Published in 2002 by The Rosen Publishing Group, Inc.
29 East 21st Street, New York, NY 10010

First Edition

Book Design: Michael Donnellan

Photo Credits: All photos by Colin Bowman.

Payan, Michael.
    In the ring with Bret Hart / Michael Payan.
        p. cm.—(Reading power) (Wrestlers)
    Includes bibliographical references and index.
    Summary: Text and photographs describe the successful wrestling career of Bret Hart, called the Hitman.
    ISBN 0-8239-6047-1
    1. Hart, Bret—Juvenile literature. 2. Wrestlers—United States—Biography—Juvenile literature. [1. Hart, Bret. 2. Wrestlers.] I. Title. II.–III. Series.
    GV1196.H33 P39 2002   2001–1053
    796.812'092—dc21
    [B]

Manufactured in the United States of America

Contents

Bret Hart is a wrestler. He likes to wear sunglasses.

5

Bret also wears a leather jacket. He takes off his jacket before he wrestles.

Bret's nickname is Hitman.
It is written on the side of
his pants.

Bret holds his opponent's head in his arm. His opponent is Booker T.

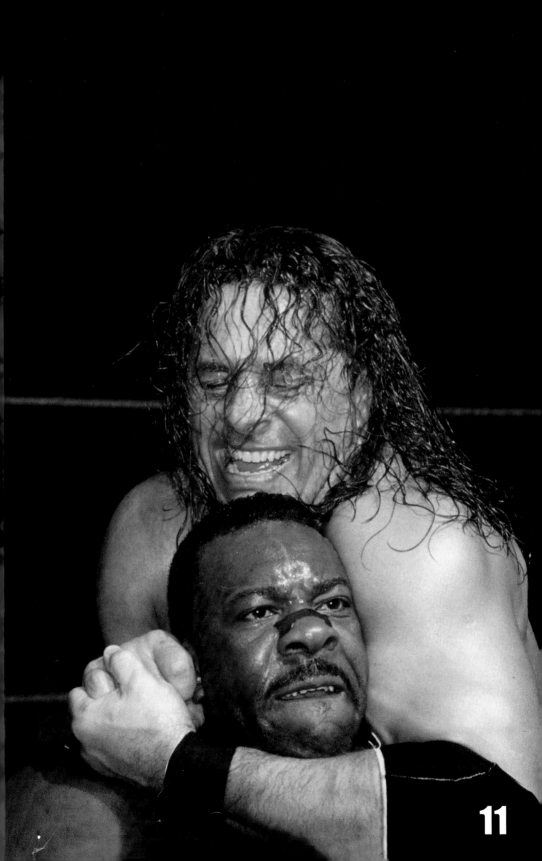

Bret helps Booker T. He helps him stand up.

Then Bret lifts Booker T off the mat.

Bret holds Booker T's foot in his hands.

Bret wraps his legs around Booker T's legs.

Bret Hart wins again. He leaves the match wearing his sunglasses and his leather jacket. It is another great victory for the wrestler.

DON'T
ONE WORD
WHOOO!

21

Glossary

opponent (uh-POH-nent) A person who is on the opposite side in a game or match.

victory (VIK-tor-ee) To have success over your opponent, to win.

Here are more books to read about Bret Hart:

Bret 'Hitman' Hart: The Best There Is, the Best There Was,
the Best There Ever Will Be
by Bret Hart, et al.
Stoddart Publishing

Bret Hart: The Story of the Wrestler
They Call 'the Hitman'
(Prowrestling Stars)
by Jacqueline Mudge
Chelsea House Publishing

To learn more about Bret Hart, check out these Web sites:
http://home.hkstar.com/~momo/
  wrestler/beha.htm
www.brethart.net/
www.hitmanhart.com

Index

Word Count: 106

Note to Librarians, Teachers, and Parents

If reading is a challenge, Reading Power is a solution! Reading Power is perfect for readers who want high-interest subject matter at an accessible reading level. These fact-filled, photo-illustrated books are designed for readers who want straightforward vocabulary, engaging topics, and a manageable reading experience. With clear picture/text correspondence, leveled Reading Power books put the reader in charge. Now readers have the power to get the information they want and the skills they need in a user-friendly format.